Ten Poems
about Love

amor v
omnia

Candlestick Press

Published by:

Candlestick Press,
Diversity House, 72 Nottingham Road, Arnold, Nottingham UK NG5 6LF
www.candlestickpress.co.uk

Design and typesetting by Diversity Creative Marketing Solutions Ltd.,
www.diversity.agency

Printed by Ratcliff & Roper Print Group, Nottinghamshire, UK

Introduction © Jenny Swann, 2008

Cover illustration © Lizzie Adcock, www.arumliliedesigns.co.uk

Candlestick Press monogram © Barbara Shaw, 2008

© Candlestick Press, 2008

First Published 2008
Reprinted 2011, 2012, 2013 (twice), 2014 (twice), 2016, 2017

ISBN 978 0 955894 44 2

Acknowledgements:

The publisher acknowledges the Estate of James MacGibbon for
permission to reproduce Stevie Smith, 'Conviction (iv)'; Louis
MacNeice and Faber for Louis MacNeice, 'Meeting Point' from
Collected Poems, 1979; U.A. Fanthorpe for 'Atlas' (*Collected Poems
1978-2003*, Peterloo Poets, 2005); Jane Holland and Bloodaxe Books
for 'They are a Tableau at the Kissing-Gate' from *The Brief History
of a Disreputable Woman*, 1997; Bloodaxe Books for Miroslav Holub,
'Love' trans. Ian Milner et al (Bloodaxe Books, 2006); Wendy Cope for
permission to reproduce 'Magnetic' (*Serious Concerns*,
Faber & Faber, 1992).

Where poets are no longer living, their dates are given.

Introduction

There is a wonderful exchange between Elizabeth Bennet and Mr Darcy in Jane Austen's *Pride and Prejudice.*

"I wonder who first discovered the efficacy
of poetry in driving away love!"

"I have been used to consider poetry as the
food of love," said Darcy.

"Of a fine, stout, healthy love it may.
Everything nourishes what is strong already.
But if it be only a slight, thin sort of
inclination, I am convinced that one good
sonnet will starve it entirely away".

Luckily, the poems on the following pages put the lie to Elizabeth's teasing. They celebrate and meditate upon the longing and pain, delight, infatuation and lasting happiness that answer to the name of 'love'. They remind us that love is what keeps humankind going, and the world turning on its axis.

Jenny Swann

The Passionate Shepherd to His Love

Come live with me, and be my love,
And we will all the pleasures prove
That valleys, groves, hills and fields,
Woods, or steepy mountain yields.

And we will sit upon the rocks,
Seeing the shepherds feed their flocks
By shallow rivers, to whose falls
Melodious birds sing madrigals.

And I will make thee beds of roses,
And a thousand fragrant posies,
A cap of flowers, and a kirtle,
Embroidered all with leaves of myrtle.

A gown made of the finest wool
Which from our pretty lambs we pull,
Fair linèd slippers for the cold,
With buckles of the purest gold.

A belt of straw and ivy-buds,
With coral clasps and amber studs,
And if these pleasures may thee move,
Come live with me, and be my love.

The shepherd swains shall dance and sing
For thy delight each May morning.
If these delights thy mind may move,
Then live with me, and be my love.

Christopher Marlowe (1564 – 1593)

Meeting Point

Time was away and somewhere else,
There were two glasses and two chairs
And two people with the one pulse
(Somebody stopped the moving stairs):
Time was away and somewhere else.

And they were neither up nor down,
The stream's music did not stop
Flowing through heather, limpid brown,
Although they sat in a coffee shop
And they were neither up nor down.

The bell was silent in the air
Holding its inverted poise –
Between the clang and clang a flower,
A brazen calyx of no noise:
The bell was silent in the air.

The camels crossed the miles of sand
That stretched around the cups and plates;
The desert was their own, they planned
To portion out the stars and dates:
The camels crossed the miles of sand.

Time was away and somewhere else
The waiter did not come, the clock
Forgot them and the radio waltz
Came out like water from a rock:
Time was away and somewhere else.

Her fingers flicked away the ash
That bloomed again in tropic trees:
Not caring if the markets crash
When they had forests such as these,
Her fingers flicked away the ash.

God or whatever means the Good
Be praised that time can stop like this,
That what the heart has understood
Can verify in the body's peace
God or whatever means the Good.

Time was away and she was here
And life no longer what it was,
The bell was silent in the air
And all the room a glow because
Time was away and she was here.

Louis MacNeice (1907 – 1963)

I So Liked Spring

I so liked Spring last year
Because you were here; –
The thrushes too –
Because it was these you so liked to hear –
I so liked you.

This year's a different thing, –
I'll not think of you.
But I'll like Spring because it is simply Spring
As the thrushes do.

Charlotte Mew (1869 – 1928)

Conviction (iv)

I like to get off with people,
I like to lie in their arms,
I like to be held and tightly kissed,
Safe from all alarms.

I like to laugh and be happy
With a beautiful beautiful kiss,
I tell you, in all the world
There is no bliss like this.

Stevie Smith (1902 – 1971)

Quantum est quod desit
(To the brink but no further)

'Twas a new feeling – something more
Than we had dar'd to own before,
Which then we hid not;
We saw it in each other's eye,
And wish'd in every broken sigh
To speak, but did not!

She felt my lips' impassion'd touch;
'Twas the first time I dar'd so much,
And yet, she chid not;
But whisper'd o'er my burning brow,
'Oh! do you doubt I love you now?'
Sweet soul! I did not!

Warmly I felt her bosom thrill.
I prest it closer, closer still,
Though gently bid not;
Till – oh! the world hath seldom heard
Of lovers, who so nearly err'd,
And yet who – did not!

Thomas Moore (1779 – 1852)

Love

Two thousand cigarettes.
A hundred miles
from wall to wall.
An eternity and a half of vigils
blanker than snow.

Tons of words
old as the tracks
of a platypus in the sand.

A hundred books we didn't write.
A hundred pyramids we didn't build.

Sweepings.
Dust.

Bitter
as the beginning of the world.

Believe me when I say
it was beautiful.

Miroslav Holub (1923 – 1998)

Sonnet 29

When in disgrace with fortune and men's eyes,
I all alone beweep my outcast state,
And trouble deaf heaven with my bootless cries,
And look upon myself, and curse my fate,
Wishing me like to one more rich in hope,
Featured like him, like him with friends possessed,
Desiring this man's art, and that man's scope,
With what I most enjoy contented least:
Yet in these thoughts myself almost despising,
Haply I think on thee, and then my state
Like to the lark at break of day arising
From sullen earth, sings hymns at heaven's gate;
For thy sweet love remembered such wealth brings
That then I scorn to change my state with kings.

William Shakespeare (1564 – 1616)

Atlas

There is a kind of love called maintenance,
Which stores the WD40 and knows when to use it;

Which checks the insurance, and doesn't forget
The milkman; which remembers to plant bulbs;

Which answers letters; which knows the way
The money goes; which deals with dentists

And Road Fund Tax and meeting trains,
And postcards to the lonely; which upholds

The permanently rickety elaborate
Structures of living; which is Atlas.

And maintenance is the sensible side of love,
Which knows what time and weather are doing
To my brickwork; insulates my faulty wiring;
Laughs at my dryrotten jokes; remembers
My need for gloss and grouting; which keeps
My suspect edifice upright in air,
As Atlas did the sky.

U. A. Fanthorpe (1929 – 2009)

They are a Tableau at the Kissing-Gate

Maids of honour, bridegroom, bride,
the best man in a grey silk suit,
a flash to catch them in the arching
stone, confettied by a sudden gust –
an apple-tree in full white spread
beyond the reach of bone and dust.

I am the driver in a passing car:
the wedding-dress a cloud of lace.
A small hand clutching at a skirt,
some nervous bridesmaid, eight
or maybe nine years old, has seen
the blossom fall, has closed her eyes –

her head falls back into the scent,
the soundless whirr and whirl of earthbound
petals, like sycamore seeds
on a current of air, silent helicopters
bringing light – a wedding-gift
the bride will brush away, unconsciously.

This is no ordinary act, no summer fête,
another simple wedding held in June.
This is the wind shaking the apple-tree,
the bell above the kissing-gate,
the sudden fall of blossom into light
which only love and innocence can see.

We must be held accountable to love:
where they step out together arm in arm
as newly-weds, spring-cleaned, and climb
into a waiting car beneath a summer sky,
the blossom will still fall, unstoppable –
a drift of change across a changeless time.

Jane Holland

Magnetic

i spell it out on this fridge door
you are so wonderful
i even like th way you snor

Wendy Cope